J.S. BACH

DANCES FOR THE KEYBOARD

(31 Short Pieces to Play Before the Two-Part Inventions)

EDITED BY MAURICE HINSON

AN ALFRED MASTERWORK EDITION

Cover art: Landscape with Roman Ruins, *1740*
by Giovanni Antonio Canaletto (1697–1768)
Accademia, Venice, Italy
Cameraphoto / Art Resource, New York

Second Edition
Copyright © MMII by Alfred Publishing Co., Inc.
All rights reserved. Printed in USA.
ISBN 0-7390-2979-7

CONTENTS

PAGE

This edition is dedicated to Charles Fisher,
with appreciation and admiration.

FOREWORD

One of the finest introductions to the keyboard music of J. S. Bach (1685-1750) is through the various dance forms he used throughout his life.

Since these dances are rhythmic, use very few contrapuntal elements, and contain appealing melodies, they make fine recital material for the intermediate level pianist. Most of the dances in this collection are technically less involved than the *Two-Part Inventions*. Therefore, these dances provide excellent preparation for those wonderful pieces. The student should play many of these ingratiating dance pieces before beginning study of the *Two-Part Inventions*.

Even before studying these dances, the student should have played a number of the basic pieces from the Anna Magdalena and Wilhelm Friedemann Notebooks, and some of the small (short) preludes and fugues, more preludes than fugues.

The student should have a "feel" for the various types of dances and therefore must know the actual differences between the dances so that his/her performance will not suffer from lack of character, especially with regard to rhythmic interest. It is highly desirable for the student to dance these dances to have a better understanding of the steps and movements. One of the purposes of this collection is to give a brief historical look at each type of dance and to list its most important characteristics.

Many of the details of the dances in this collection can be appreciated fully only by the keyboard performer—they can be heard, but their significance can never be entirely grasped until one has felt them under one's fingers. It is the keyboard performer that these dances are written for, and to him/her that the composer is speaking.

SUITES

Bach composed suites called *Partitas*, *French Overture* (both so named by Bach), *English Suites*, and *French Suites* (these designations cannot be attributed to Bach). Forms found in the suites: (a) dance movements are binary, in two more or less equal parts, each repeated; (b) other movements may be in binary or in other forms. Bach also composed dance movements found in other keyboard works such as the Anna Magdalena and Wilhelm Friedemann Notebooks. Dance rhythms may be found in pieces not so named (*Well-Tempered Clavier*, Goldberg Variations, gigue-fugues).

Two of Bach's favorite keyboard writing styles involved *freistimmighkeit* (free movement of voices, where voices may pass freely from one hand to another and passages may be subdivided between hands at will), and *style brisé* (derived from lute playing, where chords may be broken into various patterns of keyboard figuration).

STANDARD DANCE MOVEMENTS

The standard dance suite form as used by Bach was: *allemande, courante, sarabande*, optional dances, *gigue*. The basic order has something of the slow-fast-slow-fast arrangement of the baroque four-movement sonata. It is out of this form that the later eighteenth-century sonata developed, more influenced by the articulated dance forms than by the more fluid movements of many of the sonatas of the first half of the eighteenth century. Looking with historical hindsight, these dance forms were the most modern and the most progressive of the time.

ALLEMANDE

The earliest English reference to the *allemande* is found in a Scotch chronicle of 1549. However, as indicated by its name, the *allemande* has an allemanic or German ancestry, and is the only form contributed to the dance suite by the Germans.

It consists of two sections, is in moderate duple meter (4/4), and begins with a short upbeat. The tempo is rather slow and dignified, but gives a sense of flowing movement through the use of many sixteenth notes in its melodic structure. A head-motif is imitated frequently as well as short running figures.

COURANTE

This dance was a great favorite for two centuries (about 1550 to 1750), and passed through several distinct developments during its long existence. There are two types: (1) Italian. This form, called the corrente (from the Latin *curro*—to run), consisted of continuous running figures in quick triple time (3/4 or 3/8), and has a melody-accompaniment-texture. (2) French. This form is the true court dance form to which the courante owed its long and great popularity. It is more refined than the Italian type and contains a rhythmic (hemiola) shift ($\underline{1}\,2\,\underline{3}\,4\,\underline{5}\,6$ to $\underline{1}\,2\,3\,\underline{4}\,5\,6$), the latter always at the end of sections. Melodic interest shifts momentarily from the upper voice to a lower part.

SARABANDE

The *sarabande* exhibits the characteristics of gravity, pride, solemnity, and (true to its Spanish ancestry) religious and processional austerity. In its older form its development can be traced to the 12th century and many authorities claim for it an Arabic-Moorish origin. Padre Mariana (1536-1623) described it as lascivious. It was introduced at the French court about 1588, and came into fashion when the melancholy Louis XIII (1601-1643) ascended the throne, and Spanish influence made itself known in France. Since the 17th century it has been dignified in expression.

The form of its music is a slow triple meter, usually without upbeat, with the second beat frequently accented. In design, the first part is generally eight measures, and the second part twelve measures in length.

OPTIONAL DANCE MOVEMENTS

These movements were placed between the *sarabande* and the *gigue* in the Bach Suites.

ANGLAISE

This dance was written in quick duple time without an upbeat. It was similar to the hornpipe and, around 1800, the country dance. French Suite No. 3 has an example.

BOURRÉE

The *bourrée*, a French 17th-century dance, probably from the Auvergne, is usually written in quick duple meter with a single upbeat. French Suite No. 4 has an example.

CANARIE

This French dance from the 17th century is written in quick 3/8 or 6/8 time with a dotted note on each strong beat. It is almost identical in rhythm with that of the *gigue*. A *gigue* in *canarie* rhythm is found in French Suite No. 6.

ENTRÉE

The *entrée* is a festive piece of march-like character that was frequently performed in operas of the seventeenth and eighteenth centuries during the entry of dancing groups or of important persons. This *entrée* is the second movement from the suite *Overture* in F, BWV 824. Bach also composed another *entrée* that is included in his Suite in A major for violin and keyboard.

GAVOTTE

The *gavotte* was written in moderate 4/4 time with an upbeat of two quarter notes. Its phrases usually begin and end in the middle of a measure. French Suite No. 5 contains one.

LOURE

Characteristics of the *loure* were moderate 6/4 time, and dotted rhythms leaning heavily on the strong beats. French Suite No. 5 contains a *loure*.

MINUET

The *minuet* attained the greatest popularity and degree of importance over all the other dance forms. It is written in 3/4 meter, and originally was in a very moderate tempo. The early forms were characterized by graceful dignity. In Bach's day it was perhaps quite fast, but at a later period it moved back to a more grave and dignified character. Partita No. 1 contains a *minuet*.

PASSEPIED

Passepied means to "pass the foot" over the other foot and has a light and spirited character. It is written in rather quick 3/8 or 6/8 meter. English Suite No. 5 contains one.

MUSETTE

This dance, usually in 2/4, 3/4, or 6/8 meter, is pastorale in style. The music consisted of a "drone" bass that imitated the instrument for which it was named. *Musette* is the name for the French bagpipe that was popular in the seventeenth and eighteenth centuries.

POLONAISE

This dance of Polish origin, is written in a moderate triple meter with the rhythms: 3/4 ♫♫ ♫ ♫ or ♫♫ ♩ ♪ ♪. Phrases usually end on the weak beat (feminine endings), and there is repetition of short precise motives, frequently three times within a measure. Characteristic accompanying motives are also present. French Suite No. 6 contains an example.

SCHERZO

Scherzo is the Italian word meaning "joke." Its light character is fanciful and somewhat like a caprice. The title was first used in the seventeenth century in Italy for instrumental compositions and songs. In the eighteenth century it was used more often as a movement in a suite, sonata, or symphony. Partita No. 3 contains a *Scherzo*.

GIGUE

"Hot and hasty like a Scotch Jigge" wrote Shakespeare. In one concise statement, the great bard identified the two outstanding characteristics of the *gigue*, for it is the quickest and most hasty of all the old dance forms. And if *hot* means exciting, it does possess the most exciting rhythmic drive of all the dances.

In musical literature the *gigue* holds an important place as the final movement of the suite. From this position it evolved naturally into the closing movement of the sonata form; many of the final movements of the sonatas of Beethoven and other composers, being directly traceable to the *gigue*, both in rhythm and tempo. The last movement of Beethoven's Violin Concerto is a notable example.

There are two types of *gigues* found in the dance suite:

1. **French.** This is mostly in compound triple time (6/8 or 6/4; an exception is the French Suite No. 1 which is in ₵), uses dotted rhythms, wide intervals, and some fugal writing. The second section is frequently the inversion of the first section.

2. **Italian.** (*giga*). This type is quicker than the French, is non-fugal and has quick running passages over a harmonic basis. Most Bach Suites are French types, but the Italian type is represented in Partita No. 1 and English Suite No. 3.

INTERPRETATION

. . ."*For it is certain that great progress can never be made, nor the highest possible perfection attained, if the First Principles are neglected; that people never learn to overcome difficulties if they have not overcome what is more easy. . .*"[1]

Even though numerous volumes, treatises and articles have been written on the subject of Bach interpretation, one of the most important aims of this volume is to introduce the student to some of those First Principles referred to by Forkel in the opening quote. Conceptions and interpretations of great Bach performers often differ, for there is a marked difference between the precepts and viewpoints of some of the great teachers or "schools" of Bach interpretation.

Some of the most important principles in Bach performance are discussed below.

Exhaust the printed score. In doing this the performer must, of course, be sure that everything is exactly correct from the beginning. This, however, means more than just playing all the notes correctly: it also includes giving each note its correct time and duration value, not more and not less. Regardless of shading or phrasing, articulate every note with the greatest possible distinctness. Every note is precious and you must not lose a single one. Articulation does not consist only of legato and staccato; there are many subtle and fine shades in between.

[1] From Johann N. Forkel's essay on Bach (1802), the first of its kind, see *The Bach Reader* edited by Hans David and Arthur Mendel, W. W. Norton and Company, 1945, 1966, pp. 294-356.

Time and Rhythm. Time must be steady, machine-like in its precision, unrelenting—like a force of nature. Rhythm must be a living, pulsating quality—sometimes achieved by marked accents, and sometimes by expressive shading and phrasing. Though there may be some latitude in determining the tempos of these dances, (and my metronome indications are only general suggestions), they must have a dance lilt, whether they are slow, fast, or moderate in speed. This is especially true since Bach gave these pieces the names of dances, and I candidly expect that he meant them to be played like dances. Do not play too fast, especially sixteenth notes; you won't hear them properly if you do. But don't play too slow either, or you will lose the continuity of the line.

Dynamics. These must be kept within a reasonable level for Bach never indicated more than a *forte* and *piano*. I have added dynamics in this edition to help bring about a more musical performance on the modern piano.

Touch. *Nonlegato* is the general touch that should be used with the pieces in this collection although there are times when a *cantabile—legato* is appropriate, especially in some of the slower dances. Give a full cantabile tone in Bach's works and make attractive sounds. Strike the keys firmly but not harshly; do not pound or hammer. The pianist does not have to be mean to be clean. Raise the fingers for your strokes but come down lightly.

Pedal. In Bach's fast movements it is better to refrain from the use of the pedal for the sake of clarity and transparency, with only rare exceptions. In the slower dances, a finely syncopated pedal (mostly about half-pedal) could be used for better legato cantabile and shading. Never use the pedal to make a harmonic blend.

Ornamentation. Embellishments must be performed correctly, but do not become anxious or unhappy about them. If you open a new page in this volume, and if your first worry is the ornaments, you must be on the wrong track. It is a tragedy if concern for Bach's ornaments prevents you from realizing this music or enjoying it. Learn the pieces without ornaments to begin with, then add them and keep them in their proper degree of subordination. The following information should be of assistance.

In connection with Bach's own table of ornaments, which he wrote out for his young son Friedemann, and which is not very exhaustive, it is important to state a few basic principles for the performance of these and other ornaments to be found in the dances and other literature for the keyboard by J. S. Bach.

1. Bach's ornaments are *diatonic*—i.e., they are to be played with the notes of the scale. Chromatic inflections alien to the scale are permitted only in case of modulation, or to avoid an abnormal interval. Augmented intervals cannot form part of an ornament; and ornaments comprised in a diminished interval—e.g., a chromatic turn in a diminished third—such as E flat, D, C sharp, D—are not acceptable unless fully written out by Bach.

2. Ornaments *belong to the time of the main note.* On keyboard instruments, ornaments and the notes or chords supporting them in the same hand must be struck *together*; if a chord is played arpeggio the ornament forms part of the arpeggio.

3. All ornaments, whether indicated by signs or by tiny notes, are subject to the beat, and must begin *on* the beat, not *before* the beat.

4. Trills ordinarily begin on the upper note.[2]

   a) Trills on a note with a dot *stop at or near the dot.*

   b) Trills and mordents on a long note, when such note is tied to another and shorter note of the same pitch, *stop before* the latter, without emphasis and without closing notes (termination).

   c) The speed and the number of repercussions of trills and prolonged mordents is at the player's discretion and is determined by the tempo and the time value of the note on which it occurs. The termination of a trill, when not specifically indicated, may be added or omitted as the player chooses; traditionally, it is required at the end of an air or a large-scale instrumental piece.

5. Appoggiaturas are far more frequently *short* than long. Long appoggiaturas, which are comparatively rare in Bach, before notes divisible by two, take about half the value of the main note; before notes divisible by three, two-thirds. The duration of the appoggiatura depends upon the speed of the movement, upon the harmonic basis, and the prevailing rhythms. The appoggiatura is played on the beat with the accent *on the appoggiatura and not* on the principal note.

[2]Interesting evidence exists concerning Bach's tolerance as to the use of various signs for trills. The British Museum, in January, 1891, acquired two copies of the original "Clavier-uebung" Part II (the Italian Concerto and the ouverture and partita in B Minor, "Nach Französischer Art"). One of these copies contains the pieces as published; the other consists of proofs with Bach's autograph corrections. It would appear that in his manuscript Bach indicated certain trills by means of the usual waving line (∿). The engraver misrepresented this sign as a dash (—), whereupon Bach amended all such dashes in the proof by adding *t* or *tr* to them as a sort of a prefix, thus tr—. But this failed to meet the views of the engraver who chose to replace many of Bach's tr— with ∿ and Bach apparently was content! Thus ∿ , ∿ , and *tr* occur side by side in the published copy and clearly mean the same thing.

TABLE OF ORNAMENTS
from The Little Note Book for Wilhelm Friedemann Bach
(January 22, 1720)

"Explanation of divers signs, showing how to play certain ornaments correctly."

This table contains Bach's only written instructions about certain ornaments, and the fact that it is contained in a beginner's book is proof that he considered ornamentation a fundamental branch of knowledge.

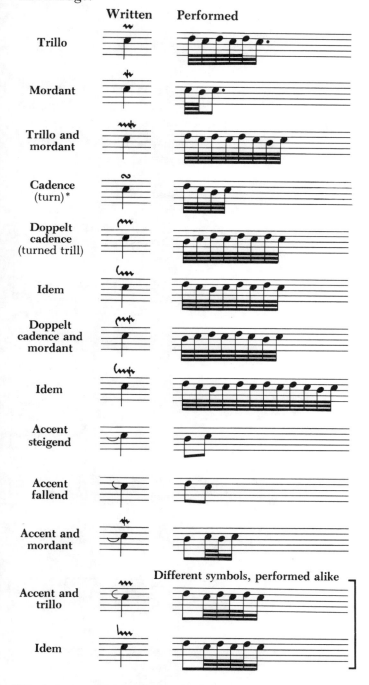

*Words in parenthesis indicate English equivalent.

Wilhelm Friedemann was ten years old when this Note Book was begun. This Table of Ornaments covers most normal problems, especially for a boy of that age.

BWV numbers refer to Wolfgang Schmieder's *Thematisch-systematisches Verzeichnis der musikalishen Werke von Johann Sebastian Bach.* Leipzig: Breitkopf & Härtel, 1950. *Anh.* refers to the appendix of this volume. BWV 832/4 means 832 is the BWV number; 4 indicates the fourth movement in the work.

SUGGESTED ORDER
for Studying the Keyboard Works of J.S. Bach

1. Little pieces from the Anna Magdalena Notebook.
2. Little (short) Preludes and Fugues (more preludes than fugues).
3. Selected easier movements from the Suites and Wilhelm Friedemann Notebook.
4. Two-Part Inventions.
5. French Suites
6. Three-Part Inventions (some).
7. *Well-Tempered Clavier*—selected preludes and a few fugues.
8. English suites, Sonatas.
9. Partitas, Toccatas.
10. Miscellaneous works: Italian Concerto, Goldberg Variations, Overture in the French Style.

ABOUT THIS EDITION

All fingering, metronome indications, and dynamics are added by the editor as well as most articulation marks. The original autograph of the early *Suite in F*, BWV anh. 80 is located at Stanford University, Stanford, California. I am grateful to the Special Collections Librarian of Stanford University Library for making this material available.

Maurice Hinson

ALLEMANDE

from the Notebook for W.F. Bach

BWV 836

ALLEMANDE

from the Notebook for W.F. Bach

BWV 837

ALLEMANDE
from Suite in F major

BWV anh. 80

COURANTE*

from French Suite No. 2

BWV 813/2

* This version is from the Anna Magdalena Notebook.

COURANTE

from Suite in F major

BWV anh. 80

① *MS:*

COURANTE

from French Suite No. 3

BWV 814/2

SARABANDE

from Suite in B-flat major

BWV 821/4

SARABANDE

from Sonata in A minor, after Reinken

Andante ♩ = 80

BWV 965/5

SARABANDE

from Suite in F major

BWV anh. 80

SARABANDE

from Suite in A major

BWV 832/3

Maestoso ♩ = 52

ANGLAISE

from French Suite No. 3

BWV 814/5

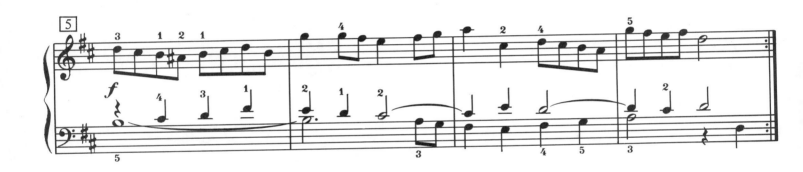

BOURRÉE

from Suite in F major

BWV 820/5

BOURRÉE

from Overture in the French Style

BWV 831/8

Vivace ♩ = 92

BOURRÉE

from Suite in E minor*

BWV 996

* This suite was possibly written originally for the lute.   One manuscript of this in the Royal Library at Brussels is in A minor, a fourth higher, which would seem to indicate a lute.

ENTRÉE

from the suite Overture in F

BWV 820/2

GAVOTTE

from French Suite No. 5 in G major

BWV 816/4

GAVOTTE

from English Suite No. 3 in G minor

BWV 808/5

GAVOTTE

from French Suite No. 6 in E major

BWV 817/4

GAVOTTE or MUSETTE

from English Suite No. 3

BWV 808/6

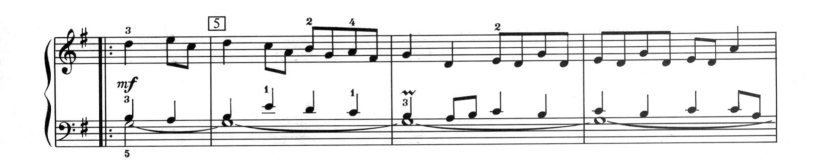

LOURE

from French Suite No. 5 in G major

BWV 816/6

MINUET

from Suite in G minor

BWV 822/5

Da Capo Minuet

MINUET

from the suite Overture in F major

BWV 820/3

Allegretto ♩ = 120

MINUET

from the Notebook for W.F. Bach

BWV 841

MINUET
from the Notebook for W.F. Bach

BWV 842

PASSEPIED

from English Suite No. 5

BWV 810/6

POLONAISE

from the Anna Magdalena Bach Notebook

BWV anh. 117b

POLONAISE

from French Suite No. 6

BWV 817/5

SCHERZO

from Partita No. 3

BWV 827/5

42

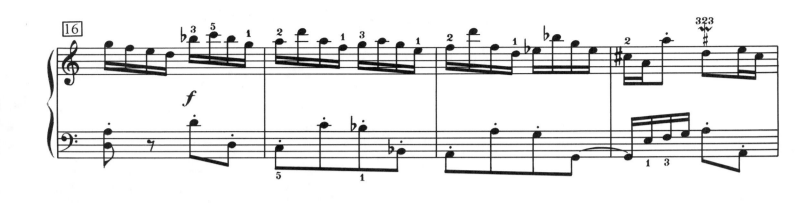

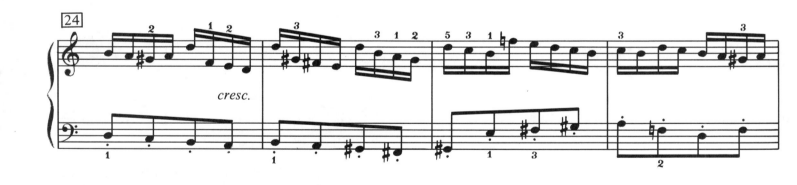

GIGUE IN CANARIE RHYTHM

from French Suite No. 6

BWV 817

GIGUE

from Suite in F major

BWV 820/6

GIGUE

from Suite in F major

BWV anh. 80